You Wanted to Know...
WHAT A WALDORF SCHOOL IS..
And What It Is Not

OTHER BOOKS BY ALAN HOWARD

Sex in the Light of Reincarnation and Freedom

Thinking About Thinking

Thinking About Knowing

Book orders may be made through Rudolf Steiner College Bookstore: Tel. 916-961-8729, FAX 916-961-3032.

You Wanted to Know...
WHAT A WALDORF SCHOOL IS...
And What It Is Not

by

ALAN HOWARD

Rudolf Steiner College Press
St. George Publications
Fair Oaks, California

ISBN 0-916786-72-2

TABLE OF CONTENTS

PUBLISHER'S NOTE

Through our work in operating the St. George Book Service over the past fourteen years, we have had the opportunity to come into contact with the burgeoning impulse of Waldorf education in the United States and Canada and other English-speaking countries. The questions and dilemmas that teachers and parents have brought to us through the years have revealed to us that, in spite of the many excellent books which are available on Waldorf education, there is still a gap in that there has been no what may be called "heart-to-heart" or shall we say "mind-to-mind" account concerning Waldorf education. For this reason, we asked our respected friend, Alan Howard, who has had a broad experience on two Continents in the field of Waldorf education, both as a Class Teacher and as an Administrator, to write a brief exposition in the form of a dialogue between an interested parent and a Waldorf school teacher with some years of experience. We hope that this publication will serve to clear up some of the misconceptions that have been brought to our attention in letters, telephone conversations and in-person meetings with those earnestly searching for answers to their questions about Waldorf Education.

Nathan and Yolanda Melniker

I
HOW WALDORF EDUCATION CAME TO BE

To begin with, a Waldorf school is a private school, offering an alternative form of education from Kindergarten through Grade Twelve. There are something like three hundred of such schools altogether, forming one of the largest chains of private schools of one kind in the world.

Why is it called 'Waldorf'?

That happened because the first school that was set up in Stuttgart, Germany in 1919 was made possible by a group of businessmen, the leading spirit of whom was Emil Molt, the managing director of a cigarette factory known as the Waldorf-Astoria Cigarette factory. As the first students were largely drawn from the families of his factory workers, the name 'Waldorf' became the name of the school, and later of the educational philosophy.

But there must have been some other reason why that group wanted to found a new type of school. What was it?

They had for some years been inspired by the work of a man named Rudolf Steiner. They were impressed not only by his views on man and human destiny generally, but particularly by those concerning social renewal. As Steiner referred again and again to the importance of education in improving social relationships, it was natural that their more practical objective should be to start a school.

Who was Rudolf Steiner?

That's not easy to put into a few words. He was a brilliant Austrian scholar, born in 1861, and who died in 1925. His early interests in life were science, literature and philosophy; with philosophy perhaps taking first place. He spent much time and thought studying not only the nature of human knowledge as such, but also its future possibilities. He believed, and in his early books was able to show, that the fact that we can know anything at all points indubitably to a free, knowing spirit in every man; and that it was possible, by a conscious development of that essential factor on which all knowing depends, namely thought, to carry knowledge into those realms that had hitherto been held to be accessible only to belief; that is, the realms of soul and spirit. He might be called a champion of the spiritual, as against the materialistic conception of man.

But what has that to do with education?

A very great deal; although probably at first more with the educator than with the students; for you must admit that it will make a very great difference in the way you handle knowledge whether you believe that man is just a temporary phenomenon of the material world, or that he has a far greater part to play in evolution than he has yet realized. We believe that spiritual realities are at least as real as so-called material ones; and that the most obvious spiritual reality is the central figure in education, the human being himself.

Oh, I see, a Waldorf school is what is called a sectarian school. It teaches certain definite views on the meaning of life and so on.

Not at all. The business of a Waldorf school is the same as that of any school - knowledge and skills; but there is a vast difference between having certain ideas about man and the world which inspire and animate the way education is conducted, and using education as a means of inculcating certain fixed ideas about life into the minds of the students. The one is something that every teacher must have, if he is to teach with any sense of vocation; the other is pure sectarianism.

So you don't teach Steiner's views on life - 'anthroposophy', I believe they are called - to the students.

Certainly not; no more than a teacher who might be a Christian Scientist or a Buddhist would teach Christian Science or Buddhism in a non-sectarian school.

<u>But your teachers hold those views?</u>

Of course. How else would it be a Waldorf school in the way I have indicated? But there is one thing I must make quite clear about this. It is not a matter of **<u>if</u>** they will subscribe to Steiner's views then they can become teachers in a Waldorf school, but **<u>because</u>** they have come quite independently to make those views their own they **<u>want</u>** to teach in a Waldorf school. You see, there's a great difference between just applying a method, and understanding and going along with the philosophy that makes that method possible. Many people think Waldorf is just a method, another way of doing things; but it is much more than that. It is another way of doing things **<u>because</u>** there is a whole new philosophy of life and man behind it. If that philosophy is not the philosophy of the teachers, then it is not a Waldorf school.

<u>So, a Waldorf school is definitely non-sectarian?</u>

Definitely!

<u>Even though what you have heard or read from Steiner must 'rub off' on the students you teach?</u>

No doubt it does, just as what any teacher sincerely believes and stands for will do the same. After all, nobody can spend day after day with students without the fact of what he is and what he stands for having some effect on them. But there is a great difference between that, and purposely setting about persuading students to adopt a way of life because it happens to be your own. One of the aims of a Waldorf school is to encourage students to think for themselves. Their individuality is sacrosanct in that respect, and we believe no teacher has the right to impose a predetermined ideology upon them.

In other words, the student must be left quite free.

No, not **left** free; but educated **for** freedom, where freedom is the ability to think and act independently, on the basis of a mature judgment. That is something which only an educated person can do. The uneducated one either just follows his instincts, or is satisfied to conform to what others tell him to do. The educated person learns as much as he can of the way things are done, and why they are done in that way, until his own judgment is mature enough to decide for himself what he should think or do. It is the realization of Emerson's dictum: "Man feels through knowledge the privilege to be," where the privilege to be is awareness of the satisfaction **and** responsibility of independent doing and being. That is maturity; and only on that basis can anyone act freely.

Ideals apart, then, you don't do so very much that is different from any other school; you provide them with knowledge.

That is so; knowledge and the basic skills to be able to handle that knowledge effectively.

What, then, makes your school so different?

That is determined by the different forms which knowledge takes as the child grows, and consequently the different approach that has to be made to it by the teacher. The child is learning all the time, of course, from the moment of birth; but there is a vast difference in the learning of a child of four, say, and of a twelfth-grade high school student.

Agreed; but what really is that difference, apart from the fact that everything must be much simpler for the one than the other?

There's much more to it than that; but, in order to do justice to it, I shall have to say something about how we regard the human being as a whole, and particularly how the child appears to us at different stages of its growth.

All right, go ahead.

Well, first of all, every human being is primarily a unique, individual, self-conscious knowing being. An I or Ego. That is what distinguishes him not only from all other beings, but from his fellow human beings, too. He does not have a duplicate, a double, anywhere. But, because he is also a member of the human race, he will have certain features which are common to all mankind. The physical body, for instance, which is a highly evolved sense organism and the source of all his activities of will. By and large, that is the same for all.

Secondly, he has a mind by which he can grasp the truth, the meaning. of what his senses reveal to him; and, because this, too, is the same for all, he can share his experiences and insights with his fellows. What binds these two together, however, and gives that distinctly individual character to his experience is the way he reacts, the way he feels as that individual with regard to his experience. That constitutes his personality, or, if you like, his *self*. The personality, or self, is unique. No two people are the same, however much they share in common by way of body and mind. This personality comes to expression in three basic forces, namely: willing, feeling and thinking. All three must be consciously exercised in education if the child is to grow harmoniously and healthily.

Yes, I can see that, but what has this to do with what you do in the classroom?

I am going on to that, but I still have to add something about this threefoldness in respect to the growing child, something which is fundamental to the whole Waldorf method and, I believe, unique to it. It was Steiner's view that, while all three aspects of the child, body, mind and self or personality, all grow together, there is a difference of emphasis in the course of the first two decades of life.

Take, for instance, the new-born baby and compare it with the child of six or seven. What is the most obvious change that has taken place? The physical body. The child is no longer that helpless infant he was at birth, for whom everything had to be done by someone else. He can do most of that for himself now; and, in addition, he can run, jump, swim, use tools - anything which you might expect of a young human being. His physical organism has been brought to a level of maturity which, while he still has a lot more growing to do, will remain more or less the same for the rest of his life. He has established the basic pattern of that body which has to last him throughout his life; and even Nature indicates this by the emergence of the second, and last, set of teeth.

But Nature has not quite finished with the young human being. She still has something else to do, which only she can do. So, make the same kind of comparison as you did before, but this time between the child of six or seven and a fourteen-year old.

What do you notice now? The body has certainly grown bigger, but it has not changed to the same degree as it did between birth and seven. It has simply filled out what was already there at seven. But what else has happened? Anybody who has had anything to do with young teenagers could tell you in a moment, for this is the time when the young person begins to assert himself. He is conscious of himself as somebody. He has acquired a definite personality of his own, and he wants everyone else to be aware of it. He feels grown up, a young adult. He is not, of course. He still has a lot more to learn and develop; but, as far as he himself is concerned, he feels himself to be a somebody now.

And this is something that Nature also underlines with the maturation of the sex organization. Indeed, Nature, as far as her work in the growth process is concerned, has now finished with the young human being. Physically, he is of a size and a strength to be able to do a hard day's manual work if necessary; he can look after himself; and he is even capable of reproducing his kind. Nature has finished her job in the human being. It is now up to him; but it is only now that the real being, that individuality of which I spoke earlier, begins to come into his own, and needs <u>our</u> help and guidance more than ever to set him on the path of his higher, <u>super-natural</u> development.

So, we could say that, in these first two decades of human life, growth proceeds by way of three stages of emphasis: first in the development of the <u>physical</u> organism, then in the development of the personality and, finally, in the emergence of the human individuality as it comes to expression in the sphere of mind and self-conscious judgment.

And what has all that to do with the way you educate?

Everything. Indeed, the whole education is built around this threefold nature of the human being, and these various stages of emphasis in growth.

In what ways specifically?

Well, first of all, you must understand that we do not receive the child into school until the fourth year, or three-and-a-half at the earliest. All *education* until then we believe is best conducted in the home, if possible. So, when the child does come to school, he is received into the preschool, or kindergarten; and the Waldorf preschoool is governed by one fundamental principle. Briefly, it is this: if it is so that Nature is concentrating the growth forces in those first six or seven years in laying down the future pattern of the physical body, then education should work hand in hand with Nature. That is, preschool education is fundamentally physical education in the broadest sense of that word. It is not intellectual. We have no intellectual program in the preschool.

No intellectual program! Does that mean you do not teach them to read and write, and do arithmetic, and so on?

Exactly.

II
THE LEARNING EXPERIENCE

Then what do they do?

Practically everything else that a healthy youngster of that age really likes doing and should be doing; that is, copying, imitating what other people, the grown-ups, do. The accent is on doing things, and doing them via the limbs and senses. They draw, model, paint, sing, dress up, act, play, of course, use tools, garden, cook and bake, sew, go on walks, play all kinds of games inside and out, listen to stories - and all under the direction and guidance of an imaginative teacher who has the creative ability to keep them inwardly and outwardly active. In a word - they **play**, as long as play is understood for what it really is: the imitation of the grown-up world in its simplest and most basic activities. And all the time the children are learning all kinds of things, not so much with their heads as with their limbs and senses, learning the basic phenomena of the world which later, as their thinking develops, will be taken up in a more intellectual way. We believe this age of childhood is the age for gathering experience directly, through the limbs and the senses.

But, doesn't that mean that the children are very far behind when it comes to learning properly?

That depends on what you mean by "behind" and by "learning properly." All learning begins by direct experience with the world and things, and you would be surprised how much a child learns in this way.

Yes, but they will still be behind if they do not learn to read and write as soon as possible.

Not necessarily. If a group of people starts out to run a race, and some of them leap ahead immediately, and exert every ounce of their strength to stay there, the others can be said to be behind. But those in front cannot keep it up forever. They must exhaust themselves long before the goal is reached, and the others will not only be able to catch up with them but to pass them, and still have reserves of strength at their command. Not only do we believe that this is what happens in the early intellectual training so many children get nowadays, but sixty years of experience in some hundreds of Waldorf schools have served to prove our methods.

Does that mean that Waldorf students, when the time comes, would have no difficulty in entering the universities and the professions?

None at all, if they are capable of going to universities; but you must remember that intellectual ability varies. Not all children are cut out for an academic or professional career, and no educational method can develop what is not there to begin with. Moreover, the aim of Waldorf education is not to concentrate on the academically gifted only, but to provide a general education for all.

Of course, that raises another question about the educationally subnormal, but I'll keep that for later. Please go on and tell me what you do when they actually begin learning.

That begins when the children come into the Grade school. Our Grade school is made up of the usual eight grades, of course; but it is here, perhaps more than anywhere else, that the difference between our schools and others becomes obvious. For instance, the first thing in the morning we have, in all classes, what is called the Main Lesson. That lasts from one-and-a-half to two hours. During that lesson, the children learn the basic skills and are introduced to the main branches of knowledge. In the Grade School, this lesson is given by the same teacher from Grade One through Grade Eight, whenever possible.

The same teacher for eight years! Surely they get fed up with one another during that time, particularly the children with the teacher.

You misunderstand. They don't have the same teacher **all day every day** for eight years, but only for the Main Lesson. During the rest of the day, they meet other teachers for other parts of the curriculum. As to them getting 'fed up' with the same teacher for eight years, why should they any more than they get 'fed up' with having the same parents? As far as education in school is concerned, the teacher is **in loco parentis**.

But what's the reason for it?

First, the teacher gets to know that group of children so well that he does not need to be continually interrupting the flow of the work with all kinds of tests to see how they are getting on. He knows that through his day-to-day experience with the children. This provides for greater economy in his work schedule. Knowing exactly what he has done with them, and what he has to do, he can range back and forth over his material in complete rapport with his class at all times. Then you must also remember that a group of children is a social unit, and social education is as important as any other. In their life in class, they learn a great deal about living and working with others. They have all kinds of confrontations with one another, arguments, sometimes even quarrels. The teacher is not only able to help them sort out these difficulties just because he knows them so well, but he comes to be regarded as their obvious arbiter and mentor. A real family atmosphere is developed.

But doesn't this make it harder for teachers who only see them occasionally, those who take them for lessons outside the main lesson?

That will depend greatly on the particular teacher, of course. The children have a full school day. During the time outside Main Lesson, they have lessons in Languages, usually two languages, Handicrafts, Music, Painting, Gymnastics and Games, etc. And the Main Lesson Teacher, or Class Teacher, as he is known in the Waldorf school, is occupied with one or another of these things in other classes. - But to answer your question. All the teachers work together as a team, and the children come to realize and accept this. There is no Principal. If any teacher has a problem which he cannot deal with on his own, that becomes the problem of the whole body of teachers; and, at their regular weekly meetings, as well as in informal conversations in between times, they all work together on the solution to the problem. This is where the fact that they share a common philosophy and impulse is so important. - But the Class Teacher stands in a special relationship to his own group, and he makes it his concern that things should not only go well in his own lessons, but in all of them. This helps both the children and the other teachers they meet.

Excuse my asking this; but I notice that you always refer to the teacher by the pronoun "he" or "him". I take it you have women teachers, too; women Class Teachers.

Of course! My use of "he" is purely convenience - or laziness; certainly nothing chauvinistic, if that's what you are thinking. There is no question whatsoever of any sex discrimination, either among the teachers or the students. The school is entirely co-educational, boys and girls doing the same things together. The teacher in a Waldorf school is not distinguished by whether he (sic) is man or woman - although those differences no doubt play a part - but by what he or she is as a teacher, and as a representative of the adult world for which the children are being educated. The teacher, whether man or woman, should be a mature personality, for it is the personality of the child that is being formed during these grade-school years.

Yes, you mentioned that before when you spoke about the threefold being of man. Could you say any more about it now?

Certainly! You see, the teacher's business at this time - as it is the business of teachers anywhere - is to teach the basic skills, and to introduce the children to the various fields of knowledge. But knowledge is not just something with which we have to fill the child. It is not just a matter of the intellect only. Knowledge is also the means by which the child grows inwardly. Whatever is brought to him by way of knowledge has an effect on him, a personal effect. He either likes it or he does not. It either interests him or bores him; and, if it bores him, he will tend to reject it. We have to find a way of approaching the intellect - which is what eventually grasps and holds the knowledge - by another path, that is through the feelings, through interest. If you can engage the interest of the child the rest is comparatively easy. Whatever intellect the child has - and don't forget that intellectual ability varies from child to child - will not only grasp and hold what is thus presented, but will seek for more.

III
EDUCATION AS AN ART

How do you create that interest?

Through art; **the art of presenting knowledge.** Next to the knowledge itself, the most important capacity the teacher needs is the **_art_** of presenting that knowledge. Steiner often said that the teacher should strive above all to be an artist; for only to the extent that he is an artist will he be able to teach.

That brings to mind something I have often heard about Waldorf schools: that their main concern is art, and that, quite often, more important things tend to be disregarded.

That is just not so. There is a lot of art work done in Waldorf schools, and the children enjoy illustrating their workbooks. The walls of the classrooms, too, are generously hung with their paintings, and so on; but the main business of a Waldorf school, like any other school, is knowledge. **Art is the way of presenting knowledge.** A Waldorf school is **_not_** an art school.

I'm afraid it's still not clear. Do you mean, then, that you bring in as many artistic things as you can to make the lessons more interesting?

Sugaring the pill, in other words?

Well, I would not have put it as bluntly as that; but that's what it really amounts to, isn't it?

No; art is not something arty or artistic to disguise something else which, by itself, is likely to be dull and uninteresting. Art is the way of doing things; in this case, the way of communicating knowledge. You see, there are two ways of regarding knowledge: as a collection of facts, or as a story. Both belong together, of course; and the one, _the story_, should contain the other, the facts. But, if you just give the facts by themselves, they tend to tire the listener, particularly when your listener is a child; but if the facts can appeal to his imagination as part of a story, they can seize and hold his attention immediately.

We are too obsessed by the concept of _subject_ in education today, and do not have the imagination to see what all those subjects really are, and should be, for the Grade school child.

And what is that?

A story! The most wonderful story there is: the story of the development of the human spirit. There is not a single item in all those facts that children are supposed to learn in school, that was not at one time the work, or the discovery, of a human being. One needs to know those facts, of course, but one also needs the imagination to be able to put them in the living context to which they belong. It is this living connection of knowledge with the story of man that is the center of our work; and, if one sees it in that sense, one can present knowledge in living, enthralling pictures without ever once departing from the facts. The story is the thing that captures the attention of the child.

I suppose that is why Waldorf-school children like their school so much, because they get lots and lots of stories there.

That is true, of course; but, if you think that "lots and lots of stories" are told just to make children like school, you will have missed the real point. The point is that knowledge *is* a story, the most wonderful story there is; and, at this age, it is the best way to present it to children. That is why the Main Lesson teacher remains with his group all through the eight grades. He is able to link everything he does in a living way with the main character in that story - Man.

Could give me some examples of this?

Certainly. In teaching writing, for instance - and, therefore, reading - we let the arbitrary letter form emerge out of concrete objects, and we show how man first wrote in pictures - hieroglyphs, petroglyphs, pictograms, and so on - before he used the otherwise arbitrary forms we are familiar with today. We teach history through biographies of the people who have made it; geography in the way people adapted to their environment, and found their way about in it; the sciences as the discoveries men and women made in their observations of Nature; even of Nature herself as a living being founded upon the solid structure of the mineral world, clothing herself in the ubiquitous plant life, and becoming sentient in the instinctive life and habits of the animals; until it all culminated in the emergence of man with the potentiality he has for selfless service and knowledge. But you must imagine this, of course, spread out over the eight years, and adjusted in its depth and scope to the awakening intellect of the child.

IV

SOME MORE INTIMATE ASPECTS

<u>Let me backtrack a bit. You said just now that the main aspect in the development of the child in the Grade school was that of personality. Could you explain how what you have just said about the way you present knowledge fits in with this</u>?

Certainly. Just recall that picture of the young adolescent at about fourteen or fourteen-and-a-half: self-assured, grown-up, able to do what an adult can do. He is a child no longer. He is a personality. What has made him so? Recall what I said earlier about the body as the instrument of knowledge, and the mind as the knowing capacity itself; but, in between, the personal, feeling response to all the knowledge that he has acquired. That inner responsive feeling being in him is what I mean by personality; or personality, if you like, is its outer form, as he appears to us. That has been active, and shaping itself, in all he has heard during those eight years of the story of Man's development. He has grown inwardly with the story of Man's growth.

Steiner used the word soul for what I have been calling personality, and, of course, they are the same thing, only I wanted to avoid the religious connotations of the word soul. Whichever word we use, it is the inner, feeling, personal life of the young human being that is meant, that is forming itself at this time, and how the child reacts in a feeling way to what it learns has a great deal to do with that shaping process. We want the children not just to know, but to **feel**, for instance, what it was like for Martin Luther to stand up against the whole Roman Catholic Church; what Galileo must have felt when he perceived the secret of the pendulum; yes, even to feel what it must be like to be an animal confined to going on all fours through the world; to feel something of what it is to be living on a planet that goes circling around the sun every year; to feel - as they do, at last in Grade Eight, when they begin to study something of the mystery of their own bodies - the wonder of the skeleton that upholds them.

You see, we want the children to have the experience (though they may never admit it openly), "This isn't something I just have to learn, because I have to learn these things. This is about me. I am part of all this - or shall be when I leave school." In other words, there is only one subject the Class Teacher has to teach, however many separate parts are made of it in curricula: History: spelled His Story; the story of Man in all the manifold interests and activities he has engaged in. By the time the children reach Grade Eight, we want them to have a conception of themselves, of Man, that can live with them as something that can grow; not just a definition, but an inspiration and an impulse for them as long as life shall last.

Just now you said something that I especially want to ask you about - religion. It arises out of your preference for the word ***personality*** *rather than* ***soul,*** *for fear of confusion with religious connotations. Did I detect a repudiation of religion, or religious teaching in a Waldorf school? After all, you did say that a Waldorf school was not a sectarian school.*

I'm glad you ask that; for we certainly do not repudiate religion, but equally, we do not want children to think of religion only in terms of some one particular religion, but rather as one of the three great civilizing forces in the development of human society and culture. The other two are Science and Art. Education should include all three.

You teach religion then?

Put that way, the question is not easy to answer. It reminds me of the boy who said, "I'm not very good at religion." Religion is not something you can teach as a subject like science or math - at least not if it is to mean more than just a description of religious beliefs and practices.

Religion is much more the inner attitude (feeling, again) people have taken toward the majesty and wonder of the world as a whole. That attitude is the essence of all religion. We strive to create that attitude of wonder in every lesson we give. It is the adjective religious, which is important here, not the noun. The noun religion indicates the way men have exercised their religious propensities at different times and in different places. The educator's task, however, is to educate the religious propensity as such, just as he would the scientific and the artistic. What religion the child has or will adopt later, if any, is his business.

Do they learn anything about the different religions?

Of course; you can't teach history properly, for instance, without going into the various religions that have emerged in the course of it. The children come to hear of Krishna and Zarathustra, of Buddha and Mohammed, the founders of the great religions, just as they do of Moses and Christ.

You teach Christianity, then?

Yes; with the same reservation on the word teach that I mentioned earlier. We tell them about Christianity and what it has contributed to the development of Western civilization, and especially what reference it has to themselves as free human beings.

But then you don't try to make them Christians?

No; no more than we would try to _make_ them Hindus or Buddhists in telling them about Krishna or Buddha.

There is another aspect of religion which is perhaps even more important than the doctrinal one: the moral one. How do you inculcate morality?

Here, again, we have to get back to the basic conception of man, which must be dealt with first: Is man a moral being by nature, or does he have to be made one? If the latter, then moral laws must be taught, and the fear of punishment inculcated in order to achieve it. If the former, then, as far as the child is concerned, it becomes a matter of appealing to the essential moral being in him, and educating him in such a way that he sees the possibilities of his own moral development.

Is that possible, do you think?

Yes; there is in every child, even in tiny children, a basic moral element which quickly begins to show itself, and that is: the sense of fairness. Granted, it is very self-centered at first, but it can be developed. You will find quite little children quick to pass the judgment, "That isn't fair!" And this is not only in reference to themselves, but to others. And, as you know, no less a figure than Plato devoted his major work to the subject of Fairness, or Justice, as he called it. Examples of justice and injustice abound in the lesson material which give the children an opportunity of developing, expanding and correcting their own naive conception of it; and in the course of eight years, all kinds of incidents happen among the children themselves which they have observed or been involved in both inside and outside of school, which become the means of exploring moral relationships. The children's moral experience and judgment grows thereby. This does not mean that they become little angels, far from it; but they develop a standard, a criterion, which will stand them in good stead. Moral laws are seen to be not the commands of some extra-terrestrial power which they have to obey, but descriptions of man's experience in the art and justice of living together.

You do without rules or regulations in your school, then?

No; you cannot do without them. You cannot create a school or anything else unless it has a certain pattern or form, and rules and regulations are the description of that form. The trouble with _rules_, _regulations_, _laws_, or whatever you like to call them is more in the word than anything else. People resent them because they feel that they are forced upon them against their will; but, if these rules can be seen as part of the nature of something they want to take part in, then the attitude becomes different. In a classroom situation, the teacher sets the form in which the work proceeds. The cooperation of the children with that form is discipline.

Oh, you do believe in discipline, then. I had been told that children were allowed to do as they like in a Waldorf school.

On the contrary. A group of children, each doing what he likes, is no form, but chaos; and children do not like chaos. They like form. It supports them while they are seeking and exercising the form their own lives will take - that *personality* we have been talking about. Discipline is the behavioral environment in which certain things can happen for the benefit of all taking part - in school, that is the learning experience. Just as you cannot have a school without a properly constructed, heated, lighted and ventilated building for it, so you must have a behavioral *building* or atmosphere within that building. That behavioral atmosphere is discipline; it is the environment in which learning can happen.

V

SCHOOL/COMMUNITY RELATIONSHIPS

But don't you find that very difficult with the kind of children you get?

What do you mean, "the kind of children we get"?

Well, I had understood that a Waldorf school was a school for children with all kinds of emotional and other difficulties; children who found it difficult to fit into a normal school.

You are mixing up Waldorf schools with schools - homes, rather, for they are invariably boarding establishments - for children in need of special care. Both schools, it is true, arose on the basis of Steiner's conception of man. Steiner, however, drew a clear distinction between man as I (or Ego), the essential individuality, and the threefold organism in which that individual operates. If that organism is in any way damaged or diseased, then it stands to reason that the individual (or I) can neither use it nor manifest himself in it adequately. He is handicapped; but it is the organism that is at fault not the individuality. Hence, it stands to reason that the educational methods employed in helping the handicapped to rise to the best of himself will be different, although the basic ideas on which those methods rest might be the same in both cases. The education of the handicapped child will be much slower, and less intellectual; the teacher will need additional knowledge of the nature of the handicap his children are suffering from, and what help he might apply in the classroom. This, in turn, involves medical consultations and frequent conferences with the 'parents' with whom the children board.

But a Waldorf school, such as we are talking about here, the kind Steiner founded in 1919, is a normal school for educationally normal children; and, although the children will vary as to intellectual ability, all should be able to benefit from the program, and the rate at which it is followed.

<u>How are children admitted to a Waldorf school</u>?

By application to the Faculty - or College of Teachers, as it is sometimes called. This is followed by an interview of the parent and child with the Class Teacher and, if both are then satisfied, the rest follows.

<u>There are no entrance exams then</u>?

No; although one of the reasons for the interview is to make sure that the child is up to the educational level of the class.

<u>And the parents are not required to subscribe to Rudolf Steiner's philosophy of life</u>?

By no means; although many of them do get interested, and opportunities are available for them to hear about it if they wish. All they are expected to support are the aims and methods of the education we have been discussing.

<u>So anybody can be admitted</u>?

Anybody. The school is a public institution.

<u>How can you say that? You charge fees. A Waldorf school is a private school</u>.

We charge fees, yes; but there is a difference between running a school as a business, for profit, and ensuring that by catering to certain social prejudices on the one hand and, on the other, having to ask for fees in order to make a public educational project possible. Being independent, Waldorf schools have to rely on fees for their maintenance; but every bit of that income is devoted entirely to the education. Students are admitted regardless of race, sex, religion or social background. And even though we charge fees, every effort is made to accommodate as many students as possible whose parents cannot afford all of the fee. All the schools have some sort of scholarship assistance.

So they are not supported by the State.

Not yet in North America. In some countries in Europe, it is different. But even here changes are taking place. The province of British Columbia in Canada makes grants to independent (private) schools. In the neighboring province of Alberta, the Board of Education of Edmonton recently instituted a Waldorf program in a public school which is financed entirely by public money.

From your point of view, is this a good thing or bad?

It is good insofar as it allows the teachers to concentrate entirely on the education; it would be bad, however, if they had to sacrifice any of their basic principles to obtain that assistance. Steiner believed strongly that education should be free, that is, free of State intervention and direction.

Education is a matter for educators, as medicine is for doctors, and law for lawyers. It is a professional public service. It should not be made to serve political or economic ends. The State should safeguard the rights of children to education; the State would also have to ensure that there was actual funding for it; but the direction of it should be the work of educators. The final arbiter of the teachers' work is the public, not the government. The growth of independent education in our time, in which Waldorf is no small partner, is an indication of the growing feeling among parents that they should have more say in what kind of school their children should go to.

Wouldn't that, however, inevitably send us back to the educational travesties and abuses of the past as recorded in **Nicholas Nickleby** (Squeers and Dotheboys Hall)?

No; because a government that was looking after the rights of its children would not tolerate such institutions. That is where the governnment has its most important role to play in education, by looking after children's rights, just as the role of the economic sphere of government is to look after the production and distribution of goods. The cultural life, however, of which education is a major part, can only grow healthily when it depends on the initiative of individuals and groups of individuals who are dedicated to what happens there. It was ideas such as these, which Steiner was fostering after the first World War, that inspired the social activity of that original group of businessmen who promoted the first Waldorf school. At first, that school was free in every way. There were no fees. The school was financially supported by the profits arising out of the business carried on by that group.

<u>How then did fees come to be charged at all?</u>

The school was such a success that, within a few years, it had a thousand students; and there was a limit to the funds that any of the donating businesses may have had available to give to education. Nonetheless, it was an example of what might still happen one day when the business community as a whole realizes that it is in their best interests to support good, free, independent education.

VI

ABOUT HIGH SCHOOL

You have told me about the Preschool and the Grade school, what about the High school?

In the High school, we come to that third and last phase of emphasis in the threefold growth process that I mentioned - the emergence of the individual human spirit in that element which alone distinguishes man from every other creature - his thinking judgment.

You don't believe, then, what most evolutionary theory seems to teach, that man is a higher animal?

It is not a matter of belief, but of observation of what is obviously there. However much or little man is related to the animal in other respects - and some relationship cannot be denied - his individual thinking judgment, his ego consciousness, is obviously no part of the animal. The cosmic intelligence that is manifested in all other living creatures as instinct, differentiates itself in man as the individual self-conscious judgment that freely directs his own destiny.

<u>How do you justify that</u>?

You only have to consider the course of history. There is not a single achievement in human progress that did not first emerge as the initiative of a single individual. Even if masses of individuals were later required to carry it out, that was done either on their own decision and direction, or on that of others. The individual is supreme in human progress. This alone explains genius; where the unlimited potential latent in human capacity can sometimes appear in one man and initiate something which man as a mere species could never do.

<u>How does this affect the high school education</u>?

That's where this individual potential appears, and begins to be directly developed. We now work with that individual in depth and breadth to the limit of his capacity. Knowledge is no longer a matter of play as it was in the Preschool, or of human interest only, as it was in the Grade school. It is now an intellectual discipline by which the individuality comes to itself, and begins to grow consciously. The facts and laws and processes of the world of Nature and of Man are something the student now has to penetrate in increasing depth in the light of their own objective, eternal grandeur. He has to understand them for what they are, and to realize that it is only by the utmost exertion of his will, and the intellect with which he is endowed that he will be able to do so. He is much more on his own now.

In other words, you now have to make up in the High school for what you did not do earlier?

Not a bit of it! Rather, it is because the intellect was not pressured in those earlier years, and because the interest in knowledge was allowed to develop side-by-side with a far-reaching conception of man, that we can now call upon him to exercise his intellectual capacity to the maximum. Has it ever occurred to you that it may well be because too much pressure is put on the intellect in the earlier years that we have all the adolescent troubles our modern society is plagued with today?

You don't get those adolescent problems, then, in a Waldorf school, like dropping out, precocious and promiscuous sex, drugs, alcoholism and even violence?

To nothing like the same extent, no.

But you do get them?

One cannot avoid them altogether. This is something which is a world dis-ease of our time. In a culture like our own, where adolescents have easy access to sex experience, drink, drugs, wild unsupervised parties, and the general deterioration of home support and guidance, our young people cannot pass through it untouched. You must remember, too, that we admit students at all ages, and while, on the whole, children who have been with us from Preschool keep on an even keel, we not only get those who have experienced the worst of modern tendencies, but definitely suffer from them. They sometimes can create quite acute problems.

What do you do about them?

Everything we can to adapt them to a healthier and new outlook on life, learning and behavior.

And if you can't?

Then they have to leave. After all, a school, and particularly an independent school, has a reputation to keep up for the kind of program and behavior it has promised the public. Just as it cannot hope, and does not intend, to do anything with the educationally sub-normal and handicapped, so it cannot with those who have been damaged by drugs, drink or the other excesses of our society.

<u>So you abandon them</u>?

That's not quite fair. We, first of all, take every precaution, especially in the High school, about what children we admit, so that "abandoning" as you call it, may never have to happen. But, on those rare occasions when we may be wrong in our judgment, we still do everything we can to solve the problems that arise. But there comes a point where both the student and the school have to face the fact that they have reached a limit and, in that the case, the student would be told to leave.

VII

AFTER HIGH SCHOOL

How do yor students fare after they leave school? I have heard it said that Waldorf Education is too protective, so that the students are unprepared for modern life when they leave.

That is not so. On the contrary, everything is done to prepare them for it; but preparing them is not immersing them in it from babyhood. You don't prepare people for swimming by throwing them in the deep end. You work up to it gradually. Similarly with education. One of the present-day troubles from which we suffer - or rather the children do - is that we are trying to make them adults before they have had a chance to be children. We ignore the demands of the growth process; and believe that, with all our scientific know-how, and technical gadgetry, we can short-circuit it. And what tends to happen is just that - a short circuit! Our young people rebel; and revert in their violent and irresponsible behavior to distorted forms of the games and imagination and fantasies they were denied in their childhood, while they were being pushed to learn as quickly as possible.

How do Waldorf students do academically and professionally?

Very well indeed. Universities and colleges notice the difference in students they get from Waldorf schools, and often ask for them. They have those qualities of character and eagerness to learn which are so often lacking among students today. The popular German paper, Der Spiegel, recently did a study on a large group of ex-Waldorf students and a comparable group of ex-public school students. They found that, on the average, not only did the Waldorf school graduates do better academically than the public school graduates, but that their intentions in life were more socially oriented. Many more of them entered occupations connected with people and social service, such as teaching, medicine, law and social work than those of the public schools. It was Rudolf Steiner's hope that Waldorf schools should be recognized as good schools by the ordinary judgment of the general public; and a good school is one that not only prepares students for life in the modern world, but gives them ideas and impulses they can work with in it.

<u>What part do you think Waldorf Education has to play in the whole educational set-up of the modern world?</u>

Chiefly, I would say, in the things it stands for; and, first and foremost, I would put the importance of human values and relationships in education. Then, in order to achieve that, the need for education to be wholly directed and worked out by educators, teachers, and not by bureaucrats and politicians. Finally, I could hope that our insistence on education being based on a knowledge of man that recognizes his artistic and religious propensities as being of equal importance with his scientific ones, will be more widely recognized in the future.

All this might be summed up in the freedom of teachers to teach, and of parents to decide what sort of education their children should have. But, we are not likely to make a lot of propaganda for this; but rather be content to let the Waldorf school stand as a pilot project in alternative education based on those methods and that philosophy we have been discussing.

<u>One final question: It is almost sixty years since Steiner was alive, and many changes have taken place in the world since then. Has Waldorf been able to keep up with those changes?</u>

At the moment, that is not entirely pertinent because you must remember that

Waldorf is based primarily not on what new methods or gadgets have been discovered to facilitate the learning process, but on how that learning process runs its course in the way the child grows. And that has not changed - or at least not to any noticeable extent - so that we would have had to revise the whole conception of man on which Waldorf education is based. The preschooler is still one who needs to play his way into life, so that his body, as the instrument of all he will have to do in the world, shall have a chance to lay down a thoroughly healthy and harmonious form. The Grade schooler is still one who needs to feel his way into knowledge as the wonderful story of the evolution of the species of which he is the latest representative; and the High schooler is still one who needs leisure and expert guidance to deal with the multitudinous questions about life and his relationship to it which now begin to flood his consciousness from what he is learning.

It took Man a long time to reach the twentieth century, we should at least take a proportionate length of time to bring him to an appreciation of its achievements and its responsibilities. To encourage him to play about with computers before he can handle a pen properly or understand the syntax of a simple sentence, is <u>not preparing</u> him for the twentieth century, but encouraging him to be contemptuous of anything that existed before it. You don't let a young person drive an automobile until he is sixteen, why should you let him play about with a computer at six just because they happen to have been discovered in our time?

You see, everything hinges on whether education is just a matter of acquiring knowledge and skill with the artifacts of our time, or of developing social consciousness and responsibility out of a knowledge of all that has gone into the making of twentieth-century Man. We believe the latter is of primary importance. Therefore, we try to educate the child *up to* the age in which he lives, not to press the age upon him before he can properly appreciate it. If I might adapt Emerson's phrase, I would say: We want to educate the child so that he shall *feel* through the way he is led into knowledge, the privilege of being a man of the twentieth century. How he will adapt himself to that century and all its works will be his business; but if we have done our job in the right way, there is every possibility that he will be able to find his place in it to the benefit of himself and his fellows.